DON'T START WHAT YOU CAN'T FINISH

THE BOOK OF

COMPLETION

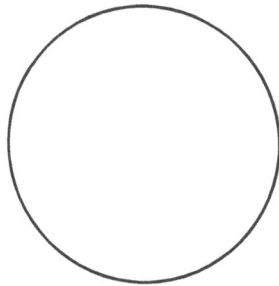

Published in Great Britain 2010

by

MASTERWORKS INTERNATIONAL
27 Old Gloucester Street
London
WC1N 3XX
UK

Email: admin@mwipublishing.com
Web: http://www.mwipublishing.com

ISBN: 978-0-9565803-0-6

Illustrations on pages 8, 16, 26, 28, 69, 86 and 106
are by Michael Nolan

Book cover and other graphics by Mywizarddesign.com

DON'T START WHAT YOU CAN'T FINISH
THE BOOK OF COMPLETION
by Morag Campbell

TABLE OF CONTENTS

FORWARD

Happiness is within our reach.

Many of the stresses and frustrations in our lives stem from the feeling that we have no control over our lives and that we are at the mercy of other people and external events. Whilst this may be a fact, there are huge areas of our lives where we can exercise control and work to achieve a sense of fulfilment and contentment which leads to us feeling happy and replete with the satisfaction of accomplishment. Yet more often than not we find ourselves emotionally drained and mentally worn out because we fail to achieve these states by leaving a myriad of things unfinished. Ideas and projects are left discarded. We have unfinished business with family, friends or colleagues. Things that really matter to us are relegated to second place behind the seemingly necessary, but often pointlessly mundane, events of life.

This book gives ideas on how to start on those all important aspects of life that have been pushed to one side, and strategies to keep things moving along until they are finished. Completing things in life has important implications that most people are not even be aware of, but which have the potential to transform the way we think, feel and act in the world.

This practical little volume touches on all areas of life including work, creative endeavours and relationships and is a companion to the book, 'Sink the Relation Ship,' which is a guide to improving the way we relate and dispelling some of the myths around love and the nature of relationship.

INTRODUCTION

This book is about completion and the very important part that it plays in our life. It speaks to the very heart of the universe and the cyclic nature of everything, of the play of energy as it expands and contracts, waxes and wanes through eternity. It addresses the cycles of our lives and the natural order that governs our every thought and action. Yet so often we do not allow for the natural order to take place. We interfere with it, try to change it to suit our wants and block its path mostly through ignorance or apathy. There is, however, a price to pay for interfering with the natural order of things and we pay for it with our health, our environment and sometimes our very spirit.

It seems to me that the conscious act of completion can be a necessary catalyst in getting our life back in order. In the act of completion we not only finish one cycle, we set up the beginning of the next and in addressing our attitude to completion we can discover where and how we are getting stuck along any one of life's cycles.

Often when tragedy befalls us we talk about finding completion. We look for something that will bring the experience, which often makes no sense to us, and often leaves more questions than it answers, to a satisfactory conclusion. Whatever the circumstances, we spend a good part of our lives asking questions and looking for answers. Strange as it might sound, it is not really the answers that empower us. The power is in the questioning. When you commit to asking questions around a given event in your life, you do, in fact, get lots of answers. You then have a choice as to which answers to choose to follow at any given moment. When an answer that you have chosen feels right, when you feel satisfied with it, then we say that the experience is complete.

That sense of completion, of having asked the right questions, is what allows us to move on and get on with the rest of our lives. The importance of finding completion is perhaps easy to see and to understand in the extreme experiences of our lives, yet that vital aspect of finishing something, of finally laying something to rest, is present in the minutiae of our every day lives too. Day in, and day out, we find ourselves in situations where completion is not just necessary but imperative for our good health and wellbeing and for our personal growth and ultimate fulfilment.

Completion can be as simple as finishing that list of college friends that you started in order to arrange a reunion, to completing that painting that you started last year, right through to finding a satisfactory completion to the relationship that finished recently and is leaving you with a sour taste in your mouth and a constant niggle in your heart and mind.

Our life is a series of cycles and these cycles move through three distinct phases, a beginning, a middle and an end. Such is the nature of all things. Getting stuck anywhere in these natural cycles interferes with the natural order of things and leads literally to dis-order in our lives.

This book is an attempt to highlight the importance of completion and to give practical advice concerning what to do when you get stuck or distracted along the way to completing all those important things in your life. When you get in to the habit of regularly completing and tying up all those loose ends in your life you will find that you are happier, healthier and more empowered.

Before we can get to completion however we have to make a start.

BEGIN THE BEGIN

Although the thrust of this book as about completion, and by that I mean not just finishing but finishing well, we have to take a look at every part of the cycles of life and realise that how you begin something is just as important as how you finish it. Many of us leap into situations without any planning or assessment and then we wonder why it all goes wrong and finishes in a disastrous way.

If you found yourself in an unknown, and therefore probably scary, situation, before you took any action of any kind, you would probably assess the situation and quickly decide if you have the necessary knowledge and resources to deal with it. You would not, for instance, pick a fight with an adversary who was bigger, stronger and more determined than yourself. In this case it is easy to see that basic survival instincts cut in and so the assessment is made in a matter of seconds and almost unconsciously. Whether the assessment is to run away, stay and take your chances, or try to outwit your adversary, your decision is generally carried through to a completion almost before you have time to think about it. Hopefully, your survival instincts are working well and you make the correct decision so as to escape the situation in one piece.

When we decide to embark on a new venture however we generally have more time to plan it. It would certainly make sense to assess every new venture, whether that be to do with business, relationships or any other projects with regard to risk factors, skill base, possible challenges and outcomes. Yet often we find ourselves leaping into something without much thought or on a whim of enthusiasm only to find that a few months down the line that the venture is doomed and left hanging.

We usually begin every new project, relationship, adventure etc. with an initial rush of enthusiasm. At this point there is no question as to whether or not we will complete the task. At this stage, as far as we are concerned, anything and everything is possible. We start out wearing our rose coloured glasses and surrounded by a cloud of euphoria. Failure is not an option.

As time passes however our enthusiasm can start to wane a little and small difficulties start to creep in. At this point we can start to feel a bit aggrieved, "*Why* can't I get what I want?" we ask ourselves. "*Why does this have to be so difficult?*" The seeds of failure are sown.

At this stage the more determined amongst us will knuckle down and add extra energy into the venture. More rocket fuel to get it to the next stage. Others amongst us will simply sit with head in hands muttering, "*Poor me. Nothing I do ever works out.*"

Unless you can find a new way of injecting some fresh energy and enthusiasm into things you might as well give up now and you frequently do.

It does seem that for the majority of us starting things is not so much of a problem but finishing most definitely is.

MAKE A LIST OF ALL THE PROJECTS THAT YOU HAVE LEFT UNFINISHED

THE NATURAL CYCLE

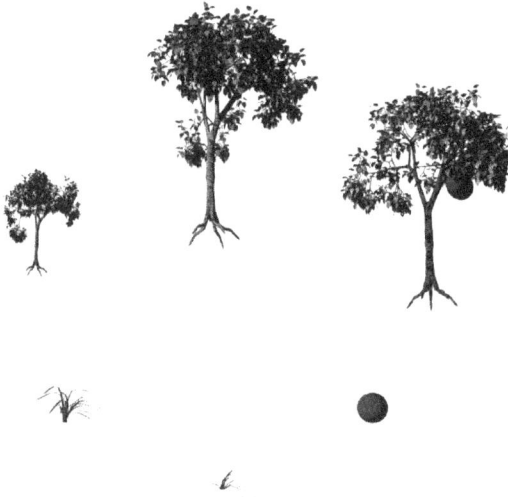

It is an obvious and well known fact that the natural world operates in cycles. These cycles usually consist of a beginning stage, a growing or expansive stage, a peak stage followed by a waning stage and then a completion stage. We could say that every cycle has a rising stage followed by a falling stage. We see this movement in the life cycles of plants, in the changing seasons, in the monthly waxing and waning of the moon, and the nested orbits of the planets of the universe itself. Planets, suns and galaxies are in constant rotation, spinning around in space.

This cyclic activity is repeated time and time again ad infinitum. It is the natural order of things yet because it is so natural and so obvious we barely notice it. But I am sure that it would soon come to our attention if the sun failed to rise one day and we found ourselves in a perpetual winter. We would recognise that something had gone dreadfully wrong with these cycles. In our lives we have the cycle of birth to death, and whilst we may entertain the idea of eternal youth and a life everlasting, the reality is that we are subject to the natural cyclic laws just like everything else in the universe. We are thoroughly enmeshed in cycles and periodic rhythms, only a small proportion of which we are aware of.

Whenever we want to create something in our lives we go through yet another cycle—the creation cycle. It goes something like this

1. Our mind is quiet.

2. Into the quiet space in our mind enters a thought.

3. That thought, or inspiration, is followed by flash of enthusiasm—a eureka moment!

4. Following this revelation comes the determination to put that thought into action.

5. Then there is a period of physically creating or making manifest that original thought.

6. Then the completion of the project. That first thought is now made solid for all to see and experience.

7. Finally there follows a period of reflection and assessment and hopefully we see that what we have made is indeed good.

If all this is reminiscent of a certain biblical story that's because it is an age old story of creation that we enact every time we decide to create something new in our life. It is literally programmed into our genes. It is so natural that we do not give it a second thought. Well actually that's not quite true, because unlike the cycles of the seasons or the plants, we humans often fail to complete this natural cycle of genesis.

It seems that as human beings we are less likely to obey the natural order of things and more inclined go our own way. So it transpires that far from going through this process of creation to a completion there are some of us who get stuck, or distracted along the way. Some of us have a head full of new thoughts and ideas but our minds are constantly seduced into other more exciting areas of exploration and we go no further. Our brilliant creation plans remain just that—plans. Then there are others of us who launch ourselves into a flurry of enthusiastic activity around our creation and then, well....., we just get tired of it. All that enthusiasm just leaks away and we don't have the energy to go any further. So our half hearted attempts sit in the corner of the room as a constant reminder of our inability to finish.

Others get a stage further than this and do actually manage to physically birth their idea. In a rush of relief the object conceived of a while ago in their imagination is, low and behold, made manifest! But then what? Often, it's swiftly abandoned, as they are already on to the next project and the latest creation is stuffed under the bed to gather dust.

Few of us, it seems, manage to get all the way through the process and then give ourselves the time to reflect on our creation, to admire it, to critique it, to learn from it, to grow from it, so that our next creation can be a new improved version or maybe bring us to the realisation that having created this once, we will never do it again.

"So what," you say, *"what does it matter if we don't go all the way through this creation cycle business? Why does it even apply to me when I don't feel in the least bit creative?"*

I say it matters a lot.

We are all creative beings. We all possess the greatest creative gift of all time,

IMAGINATION!

I believe that bringing things to a completion is not only the natural order of things it is essential. Essential for our health and wellbeing, our relationships, and for our destiny.

> *Even the seasons form a great circle in their changing, and always come back again to where they were. The life of a man is in a circle from childhood to childhood and so it is in everything where power moves.* **Black Elk**

Sounds a bit strong? Not a bit of it. Of course, not everyone is destined for greatness, and we know it, but for each and everyone of us, we are destined to create. For some it will be to create a life enhancing medicine, for others a wonderful perfume, for others a garden, a sculpture, a book, a child...... The list could stretch in to eternity. Each and everyone of us can't help but be the creator of something, in fact many things, throughout our lives. We are creative beings and if we just allow our imagination free range we can all come up with a constant stream of brilliantly creative ideas. However, the idea itself is not enough, we have to manifest it. We have to make it real otherwise we are unwittingly storing up trouble for ourselves if we don't. What do I mean, storing up trouble? Well, in order to appreciate the problems that unfold when we fail to follow that natural imperative to create and then complete things in our lives, let's take a closer look at the creation cycle and begin at the very beginning with an idea.

FENG SHUI YOUR MIND

Those of you who are active, imaginative thinkers, ideas people, usually have a head that is full of both old and new ideas that are stacked in a holding pattern because they have no place to land. That makes for an extremely busy and congested mind. A mind that can literally go into information overload. If you find yourself unable to hold on to all those ideas they could all crash land leaving nothing but a deadly silence. Even if you can manage to hold on to all those thoughts it is exhausting and overwhelming!

YOU MUST DE-CLUTTER

A cluttered mind is one that is chaotic. One which eventually, and paradoxically, becomes stagnant because there is simply no more space for a fresh idea to take hold. To return your mind to a place of calm where there is space for free flowing imagination, where the winds of inspiration can blow free, you must de-clutter and sort out all those extraneous thoughts.

GET AN IDEAS BOOK

The best way to clear your mind is to put those thoughts, well at least some of them, into action. If that is not practical then you must release them forever and free them from the confines of your mind for good. How do you do that? You prioritise. You take a good hard look at all those thoughts and ideas and you decide which ones are worth pursuing and then you dump all the rest. If you find yourself in a turmoil of indecision as to which ones to throw away and which ones to keep here is a suggestion to allow you sleep peacefully at night.

Writing your ideas down in a book, or a computer file, will get you over the anxiety of letting, what later might be an important, even life changing idea, go. If you have written it down you can always refer to it if needed. Think of it as a sort of back-up system for your thoughts. That way you don't have to hold on to them every day and you can literally free your mind for something else.

Make a commitment to revisit the book every so often. Cross out ideas that no longer hold any fascination for you and make a solemn promise to start one of the ones that you just know you will regret letting go of in the future.

Timing plays a very important part in the creation cycle. An idea has its time, its moment. Sometimes you are ahead of the game and your brilliant idea is ahead of the time, in which case leaving it sleeping in your book until the time is right makes sense. Occasionally, you may realise that you have missed the moment and the idea has had its time and it is no longer worth pursuing. We will be looking at this topic of timing and its importance to the creative endeavour a little further on. Sometimes you just have to be patient and wait for the right moment. Can you do that?

DYE HAIR PURPLE

SET UP STALL IN MARKET

MY BRILLIANT IDEAS

PATENT GRANDMA'S RECIPE FOR ROCK BUNS

WRITE A SCIENCE FANTASY

THE NEXT STAGE

If you are the type of person who gets a stage further in the creation process and actually starts to manifest their ideas and then runs out of steam before they are completed, the effects on your life are obvious. Clutter! This time however, it is not just your mind that is untidy but your environment as well. Unfinished projects litter your home and office sending out silent accusatory signals and tripping you up to literally add injury to insult.

Whether you realise it or not all those half finished projects are constantly making demands on your attention. Even if you shove them away in a draw or hide them in the shed where no one can see them, you still know that they exist. Somewhere in your memory they lurk, clamouring to be dealt with and somewhere in the dark corners of your mind a small voice mutters quietly......

"I must dig out that sweater and finish it before winter."
"I only have two chapters left to write in that book. I really must get round to finishing it."
"There's that plan for a new summer house that I started last year. I ought to get it out and have a look at it again."

These, and a myriad other thoughts, are swirling around in the background of your mind all the time interfering with what are probably more important and more pressing thoughts. All that persistent nagging just gets you down and makes you feel guilty and bad tempered. So what do you have to do to relieve the pressure?

THE ANSWER IS SIMPLE
JUST
FINISH THEM!

LAY THEM TO REST FOREVER

It is amazing how often we argue with ourselves and procrastinate about the amount of time and effort something will take to do when the reality is that most things can be completed in far less time than we imagine. When we attack a project with focussed attention and real determination the job is done in super quick time. Arguing with ourselves and making excuses actually takes up far more time than just getting the job done and ensures that we feel bad about ourselves all day.

There may of course be some projects that, quite frankly, shouldn't be finished. When maybe our initial assessment as to our level of skill, for instance, is way off, or we simply haven't the time to devote to the project, or we are suffering from delusions of grandeur. Let's be honest, that rickety chair that you started in woodwork class last Spring is never going to hold anyone's weight and you might as well just admit it and move on. In this case, the completion process involves accessing what went wrong, why you should never have started it, what resources you would need in order to do a similar project and then when you have done all that—burning it! Finished! No more whiney voice in your head telling you to get on with it, beating you up and making you feel bad.

RESULT ?

NO MORE GUILTY FEELINGS
AND MORE SPACE IN THE SHED

SORTED!

On the other hand, maybe the project that you started is actually worthwhile, and should not be laid to rest, yet a year later it still remains unfinished. Why is that?

Well, as I said before, timing has an important part to play in all this, so let's now take a look at how that might be.

THE GRAVEYARD OF OVER AMBITIOUS IDEAS

SEIZE THE MOMENT

There is an energy of the moment - a force that is linked to our first creative impulse, which if caught at its inception, can be harnessed and used to carry us forward to completion. It is rather like surfing. You have an intention, in this case to catch a wave. Then there is a period of waiting until the right wave comes along. When the moment arises you commit to it, then ride the wave of that energy until it is spent on the beach. If you miss the wave then you have to hang around waiting for another, yet it is never going to be the same as that initial wave. That moment is lost for ever. This is what can happen to your new ideas and projects if you hesitate or do not commit to the energy at the right time.

TIMING IS EVERYTHING!

There is also a strange phenomenon that happens when you have a brilliant new idea for a project, suddenly, and inexplicably, someone else in the world has the self same idea and if they are better motivated than you, or better resourced than you, they can beat you to the winning post.

SO DON'T HANG AROUND, WHAT ARE YOU WAITING FOR?

Of course, all is not completely lost if you fail to respond to this initial impulse in time. Maybe the other person with the same idea will get side tracked or give up, and unless its a massive money winner maybe it doesn't matter, but not seizing the moment and riding that initial wave of enthusiasm makes the project that bit harder to get through and there is the increased danger that the energy once released, yet not harnessed, can be lost.

THAT INITIAL IMPULSE, IF MISSED, CAN SOW THE SEEDS OF REGRET

There is another aspect to 'riding the wave' when that impulse arises. Many times the impulses that arise spring from the wellspring of our creativity, deep in our unconscious mind. Often these impulses arise so that we have the opportunity to experience something that is important to our growth or healing. This is not always obvious at the start but becomes apparent later, usually when we have completed whatever it is.

UNDERSTANDING COMES IN HINDSIGHT

We have to have moved through the experience and come out the other side before we can truly get to grips with its deeper significance. While we are still in it, it is like riding our wave, we are just focussed on the ride.

Another thought. What if those impulses come, not from our unconscious mind but from our super conscious, or higher self, our soul. So often in life we find ourselves floundering about complaining that we don't know what our true life purpose is, or bemoaning our insignificance in the great scheme of things. We may even throw up our hands in despair over a circumstance that we find our self in that we feel we can't cope with. We ask for help and then get angry and frustrated when it doesn't appear. Well, the fact is, that it most often does appear, the trouble is we are too distracted and confused to receive it. That small voice in your head, that instinct to turn left instead of right, to phone a friend instead of sitting moping, or the impulse to buy a particular magazine, often holds the key to our salvation, but we stifle the impulse, we rationalise it away, shake our heads to clear the messages and then dive into the situation again.

By denying these crucial impulses we can miss our most valuable opportunities. If we don't grasp that energy and run with it, even though all is not lost, it means that we have to provide the energy for our endeavour our self, and that is so much harder and so much more tiring. Having to provide that energy our self, instead of harnessing that cosmic wave, means that there is much more chance of our project failing.

It can fail because, and here it is useful to stick with our water analogy for energy, the initial energy that we put into a project

LEAKS AWAY

We simply find ourselves running out of juice after a while.

When we start any endeavour it begins with a rush of enthusiasm and vitality. We feel inspired, energised. The work progresses at a pace and then..... we just run out of steam, or our attention

GETS DIVERTED

Another more promising or more exciting project comes along and that takes our interest.

Alternatively, maybe something else comes along and demands our time and energy or we have not been conscientious enough in our goal setting. Either way the project starts to flag and then

GETS BLOCKED

We get stuck on an aspect of the project.

Maybe our creative juices dry up, we hit a difficulty or the muse simply leaves us. Sometimes we can be crushed right at the very beginning and our idea

GETS DAMPED DOWN

Someone pours cold water on our idea

Someone, or it may even be a small voice inside our own head, comes up with arguments as to why the project is doomed to fail and crushes our enthusiasm right at the outset. Alternatively, our initial excitement

GETS DIFFUSED

Trying to cope with everything at once leads to overwhelm

By scattering our attention, and trying to take care of all the details at once, we can easily lose track of what we are trying to achieve and the whole project becomes disorganised and is in danger of falling apart.

More often than not, even when we easily get half way through the work to be done, it is then that difficulties start to arise. Maybe the project is not turning out the way that we envisioned in our mind's eye; after all in the imagination anything is possible whereas in reality there are often limitations, or as stated, the energy for the project simply leaks away, gets diverted, blocked, damped down or diffused and we just can't see an end to it. Whatever the cause when you find yourself grinding to a halt you need

AN EXTRA INJECTION OF ENERGY TO REACH THE FINISHING LINE

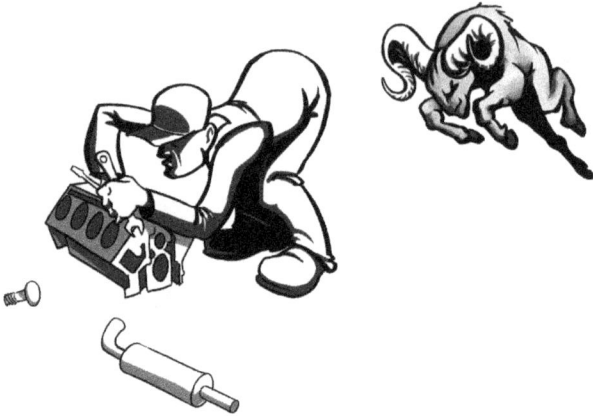

It is at the point when your energy and enthusiasm is at its lowest that you are most likely to walk away from your project. It is at this point that you need a good input of energy to get you to the finishing line.

So just where do we get that necessary energy from? Well, it can come from a massive injection of will on your part.

"I will get this finished by Friday and I will do whatever is necessary to achieve that!"

Sometimes other individuals can add to your flagging energy and give you that necessary injection of energy. They can help by physically getting stuck in and helping, adding expertise or supplying encouragement.

Even a friend making you copious cups of coffee or verbally spurring you on with words of encouragement can do the trick. If the project is work related, then your boss cracking the whip and making threatening noises about your job being on the line will also do the trick!

Whatever the source of this necessary input, it should give you the impulse and support to

GET THE JOB DONE

Even when you do manage to actually finish what you have started, and well done for that, I would ask you to consider if, once finished, you take that all important time to reflect on what you have created. It is only by this act of reflecting that we can learn from our mistakes, enforce our achievements and embrace change. This is the final act of completion and a step that is often missed out in our excitement at having actually finished our self appointed task or in the rush to start a new one. So, give yourself a pat on the back, sit down, make a great cup of tea or coffee and

REFLECT

TO START OR NOT TO START
THAT IS THE QUESTION

As the title of the book says, 'don't start what you can't finish' but how can we get clearer on whether we should even start a project in the first place. Having a definite set of guidelines and some future planning can really help here.

First, a general assessment as to the value of the project and whether or not you really wish to give it your energy and attention is a good idea. Sometimes it is as obvious as asking ourselves *"Do I really want to do this?"* Acting on a whim, can sometimes bring a successful outcome but more often than not it really is just fantasy. Make sure that you were not talked into agreeing to the idea, and check that you are not doing it out of desperation or as an ego trip. If you have even the slightest ambivalence about the work then you should consider whether or not you should really go ahead. It is not a good idea to go rushing headlong into your venture without taking time to assess just how you might achieve a successful outcome. Remember

completion is what we are concerned with here. We are not interested in half finished projects that sprouted from a fuzzy confused mind field.

If, after these considerations, you are still undecided then you need a strategy to enable you to access what the possible outcome of your fabulous idea might be, and what the pitfalls along the way might be and how you can overcome them. A great way to do this is to undertake a SWOT analysis which I will be exploring in detail later in the Strategies section.

BLOCKS TO COMPLETION

It's amazing how often we can literally talk ourselves out of hanging in there and getting the job done. The culprit is those little, yet potent, voices in our head that lead us astray more often than we care to admit, like the one that sounds like our old headmaster telling us that we will never amount to anything. The very way we organise our thoughts can also be instrumental in blocking our progress. Here is a list of some of the ways in which different kinds of thinking can block our creative processes.

POLARISED THINKING

This kind of thinking is all in black and white. In other words, if you don't succeed then you must be a failure. There is no middle ground. This leads to a tendency to take all the negative details and magnify them whilst filtering out the positive. Too much negative thinking can make it easy for you to give up. Remember there are degrees of success and you won't know that you have succeeded until you get there.

MAKING A MOUNTAIN OUT OF A MOLEHILL

In other words, as soon as a problem arises you begin thinking to yourself "What if..." Then you imagine the most catastrophic scenarios possible until, totally overwhelmed, you become paralysed with fear. Continually thinking in this way means that the smallest problems begin to take on epic proportions as you add more and more energy to them with your constant worry. Better to see problems as challenges to be overcome rather than boulders that block your path.

BELIEVING THAT LIFE IS FAIR?

An overblown sense of fairness can often leave you feeling resentful. You put in sixty hours a week to get your project under way and someone you know just gets handed that same project without having to do anything. Is that fair? No, its just the way it is! Who said that life should be fair anyway? This kind of thinking can lead to blaming and holding other people responsible for your failure or conversely turning the blame in on yourself. Either way it's not helpful.

TOO MUCH USE OF THE "SHOULD" WORD

If you have strict unbending rules about how things "should" be, then when things don't work out that way you can end up feeling angry or guilty and then giving up. If you already have an overblown sense of fairness then over use of the "should" word often comes naturally.

TAKING THINGS PERSONALLY

When you do this then everything that people say and do is taken as some kind of criticism of you. It can lead to constantly comparing yourself to others or failing to accept genuine critiques of your work, which can often help you achieve even more than you initially thought. If you believe yourself to be wanting or inferior in some way then you are more likely to take things personally and that can stall your creative endeavours. Remember, everything is not all about you.

OVER GENERALISATION

When you over generalise a situation you come to a conclusion, based on a single incident or event that happened in the past, and expect the same result to be repeated over and over again. *"The last time I tried to plan a dinner party it was a miserable failure so I won't do that again."* This kind of thinking is a great way to stop a project dead in its tracks before it is even up and running.

BELIEVING THAT HEAVEN WILL REWARD YOU

This kind of thinking has you believing that all your hard work and sacrifice will somehow, some day, pay off, as if someone up there is keeping a cosmic score card. When the reward doesn't come, you are left feeling bitter and resentful and convinced that you should never attempt anything again. After all, what's the point?

All these kinds of thinking lower self esteem, block creativity and action as well as wasting precious time when you could be getting on with the task in hand.

DO ANY OF THESE WAYS OF THINKING APPLY TO YOU?
IF THE ANSWER IS YES THEN

DUMP THEM NOW!

A Problem can be defined as
Failure to find an effective Response
Thomas D'Zurella and Marvin Goldried

Another way that we can block our progress is to focus on the hiccoughs that occur in any project. There are often unforeseen events along the way and often we find ourselves blocked and frustrated and encountering seemingly impossible problems. First of all, let's be clear

PROBLEMS ARE NORMAL

Creating problems is natural and unavoidable as ineffective responses to different situations are bound to create difficulties sometimes. Life is not *'out to get you.'* So its best to admit this and get it out of the way. No point in beating yourself up about it. So put that stick down and let's take a look at a plan to get you through the problem and on your way again on the road to a successful completion.

PLAN FOR SUCCESS

FIRST STATE YOUR PROBLEM

Make this statement as complete as possible. Using a combination of **Who, Where, What, When** and **How** questions is always useful in getting more complete information about the problem. For example, it is not enough to simply state, *"I can't finish the book I am writing."* Better to ask yourself *who* is involved in this process. This is, of course, you and then perhaps one or more others. If you employ an illustrator, for instance, maybe you can't finish because you are waiting on graphics or illustrations. Ask yourself *where* the problem is and *when* does it arise and *what* you can do to change it. Maybe the problem lies with your illustrator but only arises when you ask for an illustration without giving much advance notice and so on.

ANALYSE YOUR RESPONSE

Look at the problem and outline your usual response. Again give details. Maybe you always wait until the last minute and then get angry when things don't appear to fit your time schedule. You then take that anger out on the people around you but never express your frustration to the person concerned. Be very sure to note your emotional responses as well as any action that you may or may not usually take. Further insights may come as you go through this process so noting the details is important.

LOOK AT THE ALTERNATIVES

This should be self evident. Having looked at your normal response to a problem, now is the time to think of some alternatives as your normal method is clearly not working. Write down your new ideas or possible solutions without judgement. Criticism is not helpful so do not try and evaluate them or categorise them into good and bad ideas, just get them down.

Be as wild as you like with your ideas. This is a good way to break through your conditioning and limited viewpoints. This allows you to think outside of your particular box.

The more ideas you generate the better. Somewhere in your list of brilliant, new ideas, there is one that will work. Don't think about things too much just let the ideas flow no matter how brilliant, crazy or stupid they might seem.

Finally, go over your list to see if some ideas can be combined and improved on. Sometimes two or three good ideas can be joined to form a great one!

CHECK OUT THE CONSEQUENCES

View the ideas and strategies that you have come up with and then check out the consequences of putting them into action, both positive and negative. Ask yourself how putting your new strategy into action will affect what you want, or feel or need. It is also good to ask how will it affect the people in your life too.

Now it is time for a bit of crystal ball gazing. Project yourself into the future and ask yourself how your new strategy will affect your life not only at present, but next month or next year. For instance, becoming a best selling author will make demands on you that may impact adversely on family life. On the other hand the extra income and kudos will allow you and your family to have exciting experiences that are not possible at the moment.

This kind of projection and thinking things through thoroughly will show up problems that may arise in the future, or illuminate the fact that you may well feel differently about this further on down the line.

FINALLY EVALUATE YOUR RESULTS

Okay, you have now reached the final stage and now comes the time to act. You have selected a new response to an old stuck situation and finally you must put that decision into action.

Having tried out your new response, take the time to look at the consequences of your action. Are things happening as you predicted? Are you happy and satisfied with the outcome? Satisfied, means that the response is helping you reach your goals in a way your old solutions or behaviours were not.

If, after all this, you are still not reaching your goals and are not satisfied with the outcome then return to the beginning of your strategic plan and generate more ideas. Maybe you could also look back over your list of alternatives to see if there is one that you may have overlooked or that you could tweak a little so as to get your desired result.

This kind of thorough planning and evaluation may seem tedious at first reading, but believe me, it is worth it as it will save you time, frustration and anxiety and prevent you from getting permanently stuck and failing to achieve your goals.

GO ON. EMPOWER YOURSELF AND GET READY TO EMBRACE SUCCESS!

WHEN IS A PROJECT COMPLETED?

Sometimes, when we have immersed ourselves in a project or task we get to the end, step back from it, and then comes the hard decision. Is it finished? Do I need to do more? Knowing when to stop is a crucial part of the creation process.

In reality, even though we talk about a creation cycle, every phase of our project is a completion in its self. Take painting a picture. The first phase, which is the planning stage, needs to be completed before you start the next phase, which is the preparation of the canvas. This has to be successfully completed before we start the next stage of actually applying paint to the canvas and creating our masterpiece. This completed, the next stage which is the drying process has to be concluded before moving on to the stage of framing. So, in reality, our creation cycle is in fact made up of lots of other smaller cycles. Wheels within wheels, if you like.

So how do we know when our particular creation has come full cycle and is complete in its entirety? It's an important question. It is possible to over work something so that it ends up getting spoiled or moves away from our initial inspiration or even sours the whole experience for us.

For some of you, as you step away from your metaphorical canvas you will decide that it is 'good enough.' In other words it may not be perfection but it is as good as you can manage. For others, those with a truly perfectionist streak, the decision as to when something is finished, can be agonising.

According to Leonardo Da Vinci
"Art is never finished, only abandoned."

Whilst this may be true it is not really helpful when it comes to deciding when you are truly finished. So what does help? If you have been following a checklist for the project as you go along and you have ticked all the boxes then its done. Leaving it for a while, and then returning to it later is a good idea. If it looks complete the second time round then you really know it is finished. If you find yourself fiddling with it and making adjustments that just make it look worse then its was done and you have just 'over done it.' If in doubt, leave well alone. As you reflect on it further it may be best to leave this particular project even if you can see ways to improve on it. Best to leave those ideas for the next time you begin a project like this. This is the value of the reflective stage of completion. Each new project is a learning curve.

For most people, knowing when something is complete is just that... a sense of knowing. you can't really put words on it. It is a feeling sense of completion and satisfaction. You simply feel good about it.

"If you don't think about it, its right"
Andy Warhol

MANIFESTATION

Whilst we are talking about creation cycles it is worth pointing out that manifestation follows the same cosmic rule. Yes, the laws of manifestation do indeed follow the same basic law of creation that we started with. The difference is that up to now we have been talking about how we bring an idea or project into being and then see it through to completion. When people talk about manifestation however they are usually talking about how things come to completion seemingly 'out of the blue.'

If, as I said, there is a universal law that all things follow a natural creation cycle then it certainly opens up the question of how we bring something into being without having to physically make it. When something just 'pops up' in our life we tend to label it as a manifestation rather than something that we ourselves have created, yet it follows the same cycle. It still begins as a thought which turns into a wish, that we work on mentally with our imagination, adding a dash of emotion and then low and behold, it suddenly and magically just appears in our life.

"I'm no magician," you might say and yet experiences of manifestation are common occurrences in a lot of people's lives even if they don't always recognise them as such.

We have probably all had at least one experience of this 'magical' phenomenon. A friend of mine had a beat up old car. It was a heap of junk to most people but he loved it. One day after it developed a new rattle to add to the long list of existing rattles, squeaks and complaints, my friend discovered that it had lost a bolt.

Apparently it was a fairly significant bolt and my friend really needed to get a replacement. He tried everywhere, scouring every junk yard and car breaker in the neighbourhood and beyond with no luck. Resigning himself to failure he took a trip to see his sister to get over his disappointment. She lived in the next county. Leaving her house one morning, something caught his eye in the middle of the road. Walking over to it he found himself looking at a bolt. Yes, you guessed it. It was the very bolt that he needed to fix his beloved car. I bet if you think about it, you have a story like that too.

I, myself, managed to manifest a dog a few years ago. I had daydreamed for some time about getting a dog. We had the space and were not travelling so much so the time seemed right. Sometimes, before falling asleep, whilst I was in that no-man's land between awake and asleep, I imagined going to the dog pound. I wanted to give a needy dog a home. I fantasised that the 'right' dog would choose me and not the other way around. I imagined that he would be scruffy looking and of indeterminate parentage and of great character. It was nothing more than that. A day, come night, dream about a dog. I wasn't desperate for one I just felt that it would feel good to have a dog around the place and I fantasised about just that on and off for several months.

Then a while later I was sitting in the lounge one evening when a scruffy face appeared at the window. Looking out I saw a small, dishevelled dog stared earnestly at me. I didn't want to encourage him because I assumed that he belonged to someone in the neighbourhood, so I sat down and ignored him. When I went out later he was gone.

For the next few evenings however his face would again appear at the window. Then he took to lying on the front porch in the sun during the day. I still paid him little attention. I was convinced that he was a neighbourhood dog that had just taken a liking to our garden. Then one morning as he rose to greet me I saw that he was staggering. That was it! He obviously didn't belong to anyone, no one was looking for him and he was clearly footsore and starving. Basic instincts took over and I raided the larder for food for him. Well that was it! We had our dog. Where he had come from was a mystery. We put up posters and asked around but no one recognised him. He was not house trained, knew no basic commands, had no social graces but he had chosen us and was staying, that much was obvious. Even though he had not manifested exactly in the way that I had fanaticized, over time we realised that we could not have chosen a better dog for us if we had tried. My dog manifestation was complete!

IT'S MAGIC

Incidents like this alert us to the fact that universal laws are at work behind the scene and that we can all potentially manifest what we want in our lives. However, although we talk about such occurrences as manifestations, we have to understand that what we are really talking about is our ability to attract the things that we need into our lives.

Things are being manifested in the world all the time. People are inventing and making new items, plants are multiplying constantly, people and creatures are reproducing and so on. Unless we are a true magician who can manifest something out of the ether instantaneously, before our eyes, everything or every person that we wish for already exists, it is just a question of attracting them.

I came to realise that when things mysteriously appeared in my life, and there have been many instances of this, that each time I had gone through pretty much the same procedure as I had with manifesting my dog.

TAKE A LOOK AT HOW YOU MANIFEST SOMETHING OUT OF THIN AIR

It is definitely worth contemplating just how we all manage this. People sometimes talk about these kind of experiences as the answer to a prayer. Well it may or may not be divine intervention but things happening that are seemingly out of the blue are definitely a part of life. Of course, it may just be that when we focus our attention on a particular thing, that the pattern recognition part of our brain forces us to notice things that otherwise would just go under our radar. If you buy a brand new shiny BMW motor bike for instance, for a few days you seem to be the only one in the neighbourhood riding one, then it seems that you come across them everywhere. Did they just 'manifest' suddenly or are you now simply noticing them more?

It does seem as if giving something your full attention allows similar objects to mysteriously be 'attracted' to you. Conversely, maybe everything that we need is all around us and we simply just don't notice until we begin to focus our awareness. As I said, the universe, and all the people and creatures in it, are constantly bringing things into manifestation, yet most of the time however we simply fail to notice. We fail to notice also when the manifestation is not exactly what we put out for. It can be 90% spot on but that missing 10% means that we ignore it and continue looking. This is often a mistake. We are acting like a petulant child that wanted a red toy and will not be satisfied with a green one. Often the manifestation that the universe comes up with is in many ways better than what we wish for, but in our blinkeredness we fail to appreciate it. It remains however, remarkable that even though things are constantly coming into being, how is it that we then find them, or they find us?

Take a detailed look at how you manifest things into your life. Become more conscious about how you do it. You will probably find that you take a certain sequence of steps to reach your goal.

By recognising the exact sequence that you went through when you managed to manifest something into your life, you can run this sequence again more consciously, knowing that it will get the same result for you. It helps if you also pay attention to the feeling that having this special thing or special person in your life will bring. That way, when it turns up and its not exactly as you wanted it in your wish list, you will realise that getting the emotional response that you wanted allows you to overlook any slight imperfections in the details.

I have done this many times with houses. I know that the things that will bring me the best feeling, the most emotional connection to the place, are space and light. I can overlook the fact that it has one bedroom less than I would have liked, or that the garden needs a lot of work if these two vital components are present.

Some would say then that this phenomenon of so called manifestation relates to the Law of Attraction, but whilst most people focus on the positive outcomes to this law there are of course more negative ones too. I bet that sub consciously you put as much mental effort into avoiding certain things as you do into wishing for them. It seems that whatever we align ourselves to, either positively or negatively, is what we tend to attract and consequently make manifest.

For instance, repeating to yourself during a flu epidemic: *"I hope I don't get sick. I hope I don't get sick,"* when everyone around you has the flu can be one way to ensure that you catch it. This is because our minds do not recognise a negative statement.

If I say to you, *"Don't think of a blue elephant"* what do you immediately think of?

How many times do we repeat, "Don't forget to...." only to find ourselves doing just that! That is why it is always better to phrase your statement in a positive way. *"I hope I don't get sick,"* would be better phrased as *"I hope I remain well,"* and rather than telling yourselves not to forget something, better to say *"I will remember to..."*

It seems that the Universe makes no distinction between good and bad, which after all are merely subjective evaluations any way. 'One man's meat is another man's poison.' That being the case, we had better be really sure what it is we want to attract. Mind you, what is good for us and what is bad for us is as I said, a value judgement that we humans make a lot of and, of course, paradoxically sometimes what at first sight appears to be bad, turns out to be good fortune in the end.

GOOD LUCK BAD LUCK!

There is a Chinese story of a farmer who used an old horse to till his fields. One day, the horse escaped into the hills and when the farmer's neighbours sympathized with the old man over his bad luck, the farmer replied, "Bad luck? Good luck? Who knows?" A week later, the horse returned with a herd of horses from the hills and this time the neighbours congratulated the farmer on his good luck. His reply was,

"Good luck? Bad luck? Who knows?"

Then, when the farmer's son was attempting to tame one of the wild horses, he fell off its back and broke his leg. Everyone thought this very bad luck. Not the farmer, whose only reaction was,

"Bad luck? Good luck? Who knows?"

Some weeks later, the army marched into the village and conscripted every able-bodied youth they found there. When they saw the farmer's son with his broken leg, they let him off. Now was that good luck or bad luck?

Who knows?

Everything that seems on the surface to be an evil may be a good in disguise. And everything that seems good on the surface may really be an evil. So we are wise when we leave it to God to decide what is good fortune and what misfortune, and thank him that all things turn out for good with those who love him.

unknown

It certainly seems that we attract whatever we keep thinking about so we had better start taking more care about our habitual thought patterns. If we want to attract something positive into our life then we had better be really clear about it when we form our internal wish list. But in order to keep thinking positive thoughts and shut out those more negative ones we have to gain some sort of control of our mind.

BE CAREFUL WHAT YOU WISH FOR

Be careful what you water your dreams with. water them with worry and fear and you will produce weeds that choke the life from your dream. Water them with optimism and solutions and you will cultivate success.

The Way of Lao-tzu
Chinese philosopher (604 BC - 531 BC)

MIND CONTROL

We usually think of mind control as a negative thing. When we hear about mind control, images of spies and fascist States spring to mind. However, everything in life has two sides to it and the positive attribute of mind control is that you get to take control over all those unhelpful, negative thoughts that are buzzing around in your head all the time.

So how are you going to gain some control over your thoughts?

Well firstly you have to train yourself to recognise when they occur. So many of these thoughts are just background chatter in our lives, so they go on seemingly unheeded most of the time. You must have noticed though that when you have a problem or a concern, or you get emotional about something, that try as you might, it is impossible to stop thinking about it and just let it go. Those money worries and concerns about health issues are an ever present background noise in your head. The first step is to train yourself to notice when a negative thought keeps occurring. Once you have identified the thought then you have to come up with some way to neutralise it so that it no longer has any impact on you and eventually goes away.

One of the things that I like to do when a thought like that arises is to take it and visualise dumping it in a trash can just like I do with all the junk mail that I get on my computer.

THOSE KIND OF THOUGHTS ARE JUST THAT, JUNK THAT IS FLOATING AROUND YOUR HEAD SO DUMP THEM!

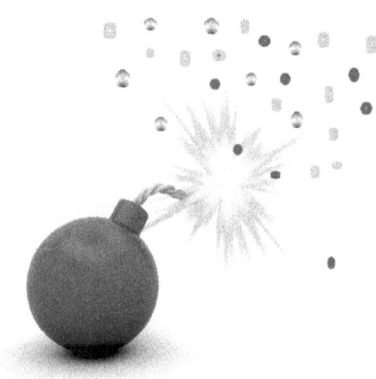

You could also try blowing them up and watching all those tiny fragments of that thought just floating away into oblivion.

If you find that difficult to do, then I suggest paying close attention to the negative thought and listen carefully to the tone of the voice that you are hearing. Every thought is like someone whispering in your ear. Pay careful attention to the quality of the voice that you hear. Listen not so much to what it is saying but how it is being said. It could have a whiney quality or an accusatory or angry tone. Maybe it sounds like your father's voice or an old teacher. Whatever the tone and regardless of who it reminds you of you need to change it. Try turning it into a Mickey Mouse voice or a Bugs Bunny voice, for instance. It is pretty difficult to take what a cartoon character says with any authority and soon you find yourself laughing off what it has to say.

If cartoon characters don't work for you, you could also try visualising a large dial or button that says OFF on it. Every time that you hear the voice turn the dial, or press the button, so that you effectively switch the voice off. If you repeat these little tricks often enough then soon the voice, and consequently the thought, does not reoccur.

Just as you did when you figured out the process that you go through when you manifest things in your life, which is very individual to you, figure out a way of dumping those unwanted thoughts that really works for you. Let your imagination come up with a solution that really is effective for you. Then you are free to concentrate on all those positive thoughts that will help to bring about all those good things that you want in your life.

YOU'VE GOT TO ACCENTUATE THE POSITIVE
ELIMINATE THE NEGATIVE
AND LATCH ON TO THE AFFIRMATIVE
DON'T MESS WITH MISTER IN-BETWEEN.
Johnny Mercer 1944

KARMA
THE COSMIC MERRY GO ROUND

There is another more esoteric way of thinking about the whole cycle of beginning and completing the things that really matter in your life and that is called the Law of Karma. I am guessing that most of you have heard of this but it is worth pointing it out here just the same as it has relevance.

Simply put, Karma is like a cosmic boomerang. It states that whenever you put out negativity into the world, sooner or later it is going to cycle back around and bite you in the backside. Karma gave rise to the saying, "*What goes around; comes around.*"

Karma really only applies to our life experiences. It is not really concerned with whether you finish mowing the lawn or building your website but it seems that if the important experiences that confront us in life are not dealt with ethically and effectively they will return. Be warned!

With this in mind how we begin the important things in our life is extremely significant as it has a direct bearing on how it will end. If you are doing something out of spite, or revenge, or on an ego trip then it probably won't end well. It all sounds pretty obvious but it is amazing how often we manage to forget this simple axiom.

According to Buddhist teaching on this, the law of Karma states that; `for every event that occurs, there will follow another event whose existence was caused by the first, and this second event will be pleasant or *unpleasant according as its cause was skilful or unskilful.'*

What is meant by skilful and unskilful in this context has to do with the thinking or the emotion that accompanies the action that we take rather than the action itself. Doing something for all the right reasons attracts good karma, whereas doing it for all the wrong reasons, like those listed above, will result in bad karma.

Even if this seems a bit way out for you, it is nevertheless, true that our actions effect ourselves and others in ways that we could not possibly imagine. The application of our energy stretches out in every direction, like ripples in a pond. Generally, we base our whole lives on the previous actions of ourselves and others. The consequences of our own actions therefore echo into the eternal future.

NOW THAT'S SOMETHING TO THINK ABOUT BEFORE YOU ACT!

Many people believe that there is often a karmic theme to our current life. They believe that we are all meant to learn karmic lessons, and then teach others what we have learned. This, they say, helps bring the whole world to it's natural state of pain-free enlightenment.

Whether you believe in the law or Karma or not, I suggest that it is always wise to begin something with good intentions and see it through to a complete and honest end. That way we don't end up hurting anyone, including ourselves, and we are storing up good Karma rather than bad.

EVERYONE LOVES A HAPPY ENDING

Whilst the completion of a project or the manifestation of something in your life is fascinating stuff, where finishing what you started is most important, and often the most difficult, is in the area of personal relationships.

So many times in life we find our self falling out with someone whom we really care about. What started out as a fulfilling relationship is marred by the bad feeling that a break up inevitably brings. We make the assumption that because we are no longer relating to this person, in fact, we may not even see them anymore, that the relationship is over. True, in one aspect it has ended, but just like the unfinished sweater stuffed behind the cushion it is far from complete. It may be out of sight but it is not necessarily out of mind.

Often when a relationship ends it has not come to a full and natural completion. It may be cut short for a variety of reasons that could include; immaturity, financial difficulties, infidelity or ill health. When it has not reached a natural conclusion we are left hanging as it were.

You know that something has not ended well, and you are therefore incomplete with it, when you find yourself thinking about it a lot and feeling bad because you have regrets or concerns. You may also feel really sad about it. In these cases, we often find ourselves running through scenarios in our head and rehearsing what we would have liked to have said and done if we had been given the chance. If we continue to experience these things then there are still loose ends that need to be tied up, so that we can feel complete and be free to move on.

YOU KNOW WHEN A RELATIONSHIP HAS TRUELY ENDED WHEN YOU FEEL COMPLETE WITH IT

By that I mean that you are happy that you have done, and said, all that you needed to and there is an end to it. You feel satisfied that there is no more to be done. When we don't complete our relationships, just like those unfinished projects, they remain with us, hidden, disregarded yet still potent.

When I was two years old and living in the Mediterranean I had a baby sister. Sadly she lived for only a very short time. Whilst I was unaware of the true nature of the event as I was so young, my parents were devastated. The child was whisked away from my mother, she was heavily sedated and it was left to my father to arrange the burial. The experience was so painful for them that it was never spoken about. Yet, it was real. It had happened and below the surface, there were feelings of sadness and confusion and pain left in us all.

Fifty years later, whilst on holiday in the Mediterranean, and quite by chance, my mother came across the tiny unmarked grave of my sister. The experience brought the memories of her birth and death to the surface again and we were for the first time able to talk about it freely as a family. A few months after that, we decided to returned to the site and place a small headstone on the grave. At last we had acknowledged that this child had lived, be it only for such a short time. She had been named. My mother was able to say her goodbyes, something that she had been denied at the time, and I felt that it was right that my sister was finally included into the family after all this time. That act lifted something from us that we were not even fully aware was there until it was gone. A kind of shadow. We all felt good that we had found her again and remembered her. We felt the experience was now complete.

I felt that it was necessary for me personally to do one more thing to bring my sister closer to me and make her more real, and that was to write a fantasy novel of fairies and elementals and dedicate it to her. It took me the best part of a year to write Earthkind, but it was a potent act for me, and giving it to my mother brought final completion for me.

Even though the person that you feel incomplete with is not around for what ever reason, or you have lost touch with them, then a simple act such as the one that I have just described can be enough to bring about a satisfactory closure. Rituals are powerful acts that have an impact on both our conscious and subconscious minds. Finding a ritual that has power and meaning for you is a good way to help bring about completion. For instance, if you feel that you have many things left unsaid, and it is not possible to say them directly to the person involved, then it can help to write them down. Pour out everything, all the things that you wish you could have said to them face to face onto the page. Make sure that you write from your heart without blame or malice and then utilise the natural elements around us to carry your words away so that you free of them.

AIR FIRE WATER EARTH

Utilising the natural elements, you then have the choice of burning the paper on which you wrote and watching the smoke take the words away, or maybe you feel happier about burying the paper in the earth in a significant place or setting it afloat in a small paper boat to send it downstream to be carried away to sea. Conversely, you could tie it to a balloon or paper lantern and cast it adrift in the air. This way all those thoughts and feelings that you have been hanging on to for years can be released. You have said everything that it is possible to say. You could say a prayer to send them on their way if that feels right.

Often we are left with feelings of guilt after a separation. Guilt is a very self destructive emotion so either let it go, as it is serving no one, or do something about it by an act of recompense. If the guilt is around something that you feel you swindled the person out of, then give it back. If they are no longer around then a donation of an appropriate amount to a charity that they were fond of can help. If you feel that you hurt them emotionally in some way then finding something that will atone for that is invaluable.

STARTING YOUR HAPPY ENDING

Starting your happy ending means looking at four basic behavioural skills, they are; taking responsibility, apologising, forgiving and forgetting. Sometimes it will be necessary for you to take responsibility for your actions and apologise, sometimes forgiving and forgetting is what is called. Yes, selective amnesia can be a good thing! Occasionally, we might find ourselves having to do all four which initially sounds like a tall order but believe me it's worth it in the long run.

TAKE RESPONSIBILITY FOR WHAT YOU DID WRONG

The first step on the road to completion can be the hardest as it is a big first step. Taking responsibility for your part in what went wrong between you means that you acknowledge the hurt you caused the other person. Often we do things unconsciously and through habit and we don't realise the effect that they can be having. This is an opportunity to take a good look at all your behavioural patterns and decide which ones do not serve you or others and make a vow to change them.

APOLOGISE

When you do so, be sure to make it so the apology is not about you doing something to make yourself feel better but rather to genuinely say how sorry you are about the hurt that you caused the other person. Make sure that it is sincere. People know when you just going through the motions and the apology is just empty words. If you have taken responsibility for your part in what went wrong then your apology will be sincere and if you can also give a pledge to do things differently from here on in, that will make the apology more meaningful for both of you. Hopefully, your apology will be accepted but even if your apology is ignored or rejected, the important thing is that you did it.

FORGIVE

A genuine act of forgiveness means that you have to let go of all the anger and hurt that you feel towards a person. You have to be able to forgive them even when the response from the person to your act of forgiveness is not what you want. In other words, don't expect them to turn around and say everything is now alright just because you ask for their forgiveness. DO IT NO MATTER WHAT THE OUTCOME.

FORGET

Forgive and forget, these two words seem to go hand in hand. *"I will forgive you,"* we often say, *"but I'll never forget what you did."* If this is the case then guess what? You have not truly forgiven.You have just paid lip service to the concept. Often, we will not forgive a person because we can't forget what they have done and want to keep punishing them for what they did. Continuing to blame them and reliving the feelings of hurt and anger that you feel is designed to keep them in a constant state of guilt. Strangely, we can continue to keep this up even when the person is long gone. How ridiculous is that? When we let go of the desire to punish and make them suffer then we can move to forgiveness and forgetfulness.

When you truly forgive then you should make a vow not to talk to them about the situation ever again or indeed anyone else. Repeating it keeps it alive and feeds any emotion that you may still be harbouring.

FORGIVE AND FORGET
GO HAND IN HAND

WHEN IS A RELATIONSHIP FINISHED?

Completing a relationship is one thing, however, in many cases the difficulty is not in achieving a good completion but acknowledging that the relationship has indeed finished in the first place. In truth, I believe that we all know when a relationship is over, admitting it to ourselves is another matter. Just in case you are under any illusion about the relationship that you are currently in, or you are having difficulty admitting that it might really be over, read on.

WHAT'S IN IT FOR ME?

This is a good question to ask yourself. If your relationship seems one-sided, that is one of you is getting more from the relationship than the other then that's a big clue, for one of you at least, that it is not working. This kind of imbalance can lead to resentment. You need to honest about whether your needs are being met. Sometimes your partner can feel significantly stronger about the relationship than you do. This can rub off on you so that in their presence you can feel that, *'This is the right thing for me.'* However, if, when the two of you are apart, you feel less intense or indifferent about the relationship, then you are not truly relating and you are not being honest with yourself. The relationship is finished.

HOW IS IT FOR ME?

Relating to someone should be fun and enjoyable for a good percentage of the time that you spend with each other, otherwise what is the point? When it just isn't fun to be around each other any more, when niggles and disgruntlements are an every day occurrence, and when there is a lack of willingness in one or both partners to sort out the underlying problems, then it is over.

A LITTLE RESPECT

When you neither one of you is feeling appreciated or respected, and may even feel damaged by your relating experience together then the writing is on the wall.

BEHAVE!

When you can no longer tolerate the other person's behaviour and he or she is unwilling to change it then the finishing line is in sight.

IS THE FUTURE ROSY?

If you visualize your future together by taking your present situation with this person and fast forwarding it into say 5, 10 or 15 years time, and you are disturbed by the image, then it is time to get out. There is an old saying that goes something along the lines of *"If you want to know your future, just look at your past."* Trite as that may sound it is true. If you do nothing to change the way that you relate then the way you have been relating is the way you will continue to relate.

WHY WE DON'T END IT

There are many reasons why we fail to end a relationship that we know is no longer working for us. Let's take a look at some of them.

FEAR OF FAILURE

Often, we correlate the ending of a relationship with failure. We say, *"I've failed in this relationship"* or *"My marriage has failed."* No one likes to feel a failure and no one likes to feel they might be blamed for failing. Somehow we feel that we are being judged and found wanting if we decide to leave or terminate a relationships so we decide to stay even though that might not be what we truly want.

SOCIAL AND PEER PRESSURE

This can link into our fear and our conditioning about failure. We feel obliged to act in a certain way because we are overly concerned with what people might think of us. This social and peer pressure plays a big part in influencing you when you consider your options. The fear of shattering your public image, or maybe losing your friends, often keeps you in a situation that you would rather walk away from. Again there is a need to be honest and real with yourself if you find yourself caught in this self made trap.

NOT BEING HONEST

It's important to clearly understand our needs in a relationship and the qualities that we want in a partner. Sometimes it is hard to be absolutely honest, and so we find our self compromising on the qualities that are essential to us. Typically, if a quality which matters deeply to us is missing in our partner then we can begin to think that they will gain this quality just by being with us or, if not, that we have the ability to bring about the desired change in them. This is delusional thinking and is especially true for women, who often hang in there in the misguided hope that all will eventually be well. The truth is, we can't make people change, so wake up and realise that it's no good wishing and hoping that they will.

Needs can be taken to an extreme and we should always be realistic in our expectations. Being honest is also about recognising our own, sometimes not so endearing, qualities.

FEAR AND GUILT

Sometimes we stay in relationships that we know aren't necessarily right for us because we are afraid. We fear loneliness, criticism, lack of support, we fear hurting our partner, and we fear having to deal with uncomfortable situations and the repercussions of our leaving. We even fear that we will never love or be loved again.

We feel guilt when we recognize that we are not being honest with ourselves and thus being tacitly dishonest and unfair to our partners. Our partners can even lay a guilt trip on us as a ploy to get us to stay. *"How could you possibly do this to me?"* We then feel obliged to stay because our partner is so dependent. A needy partner taps into our feelings of guilt about leaving them but we then end up resenting them and this poisons the relationship even more.

61

LOSS OF FRIENDSHIP

Traditionally, when relationships end, we tend to cut the person right out of our life. When we feel hurt and over emotional, it is often easier to shut the person out as if they no longer exist than to deal with the emotions that have arisen. Later we can find ourselves swamped in grief as this person has literally become 'dead' to us.

The other thing I often hear people say when a relationship is about to finish is, *"But I will lose my best friend."* If you walk away this may be true but when the hurt has healed, and if we can come to a place of resolution and completion within ourselves, then it may be possible to continue to relate to this other person as a friend.

CONFUSION

The reality is that often all these things get entangled together and it can become really problematic to unravel them. All this entanglement leads to confusion and it is impossible to come to the right decision when we are confused. Sometimes we need space to allow the mists of confusion to clear and time to allow us to tap into our true feelings before we decide to act.

END IT RIGHT

Finishing a relationship and feeling complete about it is, in large part, all about ending it in a good way. When you have to tell the person that you are relating to that you have come to the end of the road and the relationship is over for you, just blurting it out or shouting it out in a fit of pique is definitely not a good way. Here are a few simple ideas that will help if, and when, you have to break the bad news.

TIMING IS EVERYTHING

If the person is feeling pressurised, emotional and distracted then it is not a good time to have a conversation. Starting a conversation while the person is cooking a meal, sorting out household bills or watching their favourite programme on television is a bad idea. Much better to suggest that you have something important to discuss and set a mutually agreeable time for it to happen.

SET A LIMIT

Often conversations of this kind can go on and on, and round and round, which is not helpful. Give yourself enough time to discuss all the issues but not so much time that you continuously go over old ground. Digging up old experiences and conversations can be painful and damaging.

FORWARNED

Let them know that this is going to be a difficult conversation. This sets the scene and allows both of you to acknowledge the seriousness of the conversation and that, because of this, what you have to say may not always come out very coherently. It is often hard to be congruent when we are talking about something that has a lot of emotion tied up in it.

BE CLEAR

State your reasons for ending the relationship as clearly and as gently as you can. Avoid blaming and finger pointing. In fact, avoid the 'You' word altogether if you can. Keeping the conversation to "*I feel*" or "*my experience*" is less threatening and emotive and, in truth, we can only ever speak for ourselves. Keep what you have to say, short. Endless explanations do not help and only add confusion.

REPEAT

Be prepared to repeat your reasons for wanting to end things but without too much expansion. If you expand on the topic too much it is easy to fall into making excuses or blaming.

STAY CALM

Do not start a row, even if you feel angry and hurt. If things start to escalate, take time out if necessary for you both to calm down and then continue. Remember that the more emotional someone is, the less able they are to take things in. Do not expect them to think or react rationally.

Accept that possibly nothing you can say will make it better. However you may like to consider what I said before, and that is, taking responsibility for your part in the relationship, apologising where necessary and forgiving or asking for forgiveness if appropriate.

THINGS TO DEFINITELY AVOID

All too often when things start to go wrong in a relationship we panic, and end up finishing it in a totally inappropriate and damaging way. The following are things that we should definitely avoid.

Becoming antagonistic in the hope that your partner will dump you

Ending the relationship during a telephone conversation

Suddenly cutting off all contact without first giving an explanation

Texting, emailing or leaving a voice message

Revealing your intention to end the relationship to other people before your partner knows

Antagonising your partner then ending in the middle of a row

Initiating an affair

Getting someone else to pass the message on

Halting the decision to end it, when you really know it is over

Terminating a relationship in a public place, unless you feel unsafe

All this may sound pretty juvenile and that's because it is. Any of these ways of finishing the relationship that you are in, means that you are coming from a fearful and immature place.

So grow up, take responsibility and

DO IT RIGHT!

NO REGRETS

Making sure that you complete your personal relationships and projects in a good way, such that you satisfied with the outcome and feel emotionally free from them, is important so that you don't put yourself through the hell of looking back on your life with regret. Regrets get us nowhere but they tie up our emotions and make us sad.

YOU KNOW YOU HAVE REGRETS WHEN

YOU KEEP RELIVING A SITUATION

When we have regrets we often find ourselves dwelling on them. The more we dwell on them the bigger and more significant they can seem. Often we can find ourselves going over the event in our minds but changing the scenario to a different outcome. When things have ended badly we tend to end up talking about them incessantly to anyone who will listen. This only works for a while as pretty soon your friends are going to tired of the same old story and start avoiding you.

WHAT HAPPENED BECOMES A BURDEN THAT INTERFERES WITH YOUR CURRENT HAPPINESS

Once you know the source of your regret then either do something about it to bring completion or modify your behaviour so that you don't do the same thing again and compound the problem. Repeated regrets are going to make you even more unhappy. Take the opportunity to learn from past regrets, adapt and move on. By acknowledging the things that we have regrets about and resolving them we can learn from the experience and this gives us an opportunity to grow and mature.

If we fail to complete our relationships appropriately and do not find closure, or leave our projects unfinished, then we will find ourselves in the same situation again and again until we have learned the lesson of completion. Better to do it right each time and avoid unnecessary and painful replays.

IT RESTRICTS YOUR FUTURE PLANNING

By not dwelling on the past incessantly, we feel more capable and able to take charge of our lives better. So, you can stop living in the past and move confidently into the future.

BEING COMPLETE IN YOURSELF

So far we have been looking at ways in which you can complete those ideas, projects and relationships in your life, but what about feeling complete in yourself? Do we even know what it feels like to be complete in ourselves? So often in our life we look to other people to complete us. We find someone special, our soul mate even. We say they complete us, or make us whole, as if there is some gap or emptiness in us that needs to be filled and they are the one to do it. This puts a tremendous pressure on this poor soul because whilst it may feel like that, common sense tells us that no-one person can complete us. No relationship is going to stand the test of time under such pressure.

Ideally, we have to feel complete in ourselves. What exactly does that mean and why is it so important? Well, feeling complete in ourselves often involves acknowledging all the different aspects of ourselves, some of which may well be activated or highlighted by another individual, but belong solely to us. Once we have acknowledged them, we have to begin to feel good about them and that requires a process of reconciliation and integration. This means that we have to come to terms with the seemingly conflicting parts of our self and that can take lots of self reflection and work.

Each of us is a complicated mix of contrasting, and sometimes conflicting, behaviours, beliefs and mind patterns. To be okay with these we have stop denying some aspects of our self while glorifying others and find a way to reconcile what can seem like a duel or conflict going on within us. It goes without saying that if we have behaviours that are detrimental to ourselves and to others then it is wise to give them up and substitute more positive ones. Being in relationship to another person is fertile ground for highlighting all our behaviours and is an invaluable training ground for self knowledge and self growth. That other person can mirror our behaviours so that we can get really clear about them, giving us a chance for change and development.

The behaviours that we have that shape our personality are learned at an early age. Because they are learned, they can be un-learned, and more positive behaviours substituted instead. We often resist changing because we fear that we will not know ourselves anymore if we change. That is, of course, ridiculous and who says that we have to change everything about ourselves anyway. That would most definitely be throwing the baby out with the bath water. By careful self reflection we can maintain those behaviours that serve us and just eliminate those that cause us to be unhappy about ourselves. Remember we are not our behaviours but it is our behaviours that most people react to. Change your behaviour and you will elicit different responses from the people around you.

Only when we feel good about ourselves and can act independently in the world, can we be said to be truly complete.

BEING COMPLETE IN YOURSELF MEANS

You actually enjoy doing things on your own. You don't spend time feeling lonely. In fact, whether you are single or in a relationship, you cherish your time alone and are happy with your own company.

You can be around other couples by yourself without feeling jealous or sad if you don't have a partner in your life.

If you are single, you do not constantly obsess about being in a relationship. Whilst the idea of being in a relationship sounds wonderful, it is not something that drives you or occupies your every waking moment. If you are in a partnership, it does not consume your daily thoughts or define your activities. It is vital that you can still be your own person and maintain your independence.

You have a clear sense of who you are and what your beliefs and values are. So much so that another person would not be able to sway you or persuade you to give up or change the things that matter to you the most in life.

You realize you are responsible for your own happiness and do not look to anyone else to make you feel a certain way. Nor do you blame others for any unhappiness in your life. In this way, you can enjoy another person exactly as they are without wanting to change them to suit you.

Once you feel complete in yourself you are ideally placed to fulfil your potential. That is, you are ready to complete the tasks that are important to you in this life because you are no longer preoccupied with the dross. When you are able to do this you can no longer look back over your life and see it filled with regrets and guilt and that's a big PLUS!

What does it actually mean to fulfil your potential? It means being the best you can be by developing the gifts and skills that you posses and then building on them so that you are continuously growing and developing to meet Life's challenges. I believe it also means stepping into your power and that involves finding out who you really are and then honestly expressing that in the world. It is more about how you do things than what you do. How you achieve something is what will give you personal satisfaction and enjoyment.

Now, that all sounds like a big task, but there are some tips that you can follow to guide you through the work you have to do in order to realise your full potential and complete your Life's work.

Don't waste time wishing things were different. Start from where you are in this present moment. Acknowledge what your skills are and what works for you already and then build on them.

Focusing on the gifts you have will help you to expand on them. Some people argue that you should focus more on your weaknesses, however, what's the point of spending time and energy on your weaknesses, which will make you weaker, more miserable, and less able to cope, when you could be better occupied focussing on your gifts. The only proviso to this is, if some weakness you have is actually spoiling your strengths, then change it.

Automatic habits are constrictive and they hold you back. They encourage you to repeat the past, whether or not it still works for you. Make sure that you hang on the good aspects and dump the others. Make a note of any habits that block your progress or lead you up dead ends and work to let them go. That way you can make conscious choices. One way to be in charge of your future, your destiny, is to be clear about the choices that you make. Don't make choices out of habit, or desperation and don't make major decisions when you are in a bad place emotionally. Making conscious choices means that you are in control.

Realizing your potential always demands learning. Learning is a life long activity that broadens your viewpoints, multiplies your options and increases your choices.

REMEMBER POTENTIAL IS NOT FIXED.

It is not a question of you either having 'IT' or not. Keep working on yourself and you can be who you want to be.

COMPLETING YOUR DESTINY

When we were talking about wheels within wheels earlier and how life is composed of many, many cycles, reaching your destiny is perhaps the biggest cycle of all and the ultimate completion in life.

Most people are familiar with the concept of destiny or a life purpose, however most people are unsure as to what their destiny might be. Often they assume that it has to be some monumental task, such as saving the planet or feeding the world whereas it is often much more simple than that. Let's look an example given by Buckminster Fuller, one of the greatest thinkers and inventors of the twentieth century, and that is the life purpose of the humble honey bee. Bees are essential to human life on Earth. They cross pollinate plants so as to produce fruits and seeds for us to eat. It has been said that if the bee population died out then human life would be extinct in five short years. Do you think the bee gets up each morning, its mind weighed down with the enormity of its task and its responsibility? No, collecting nectar to make into honey is all the bee is concerned with. The honey bee's true purpose in life can be said to be pollinating flowers and yet the bee is unaware of the huge importance of its simple daily task and is only concerned with the work at hand, which it performs perfectly. Likewise, what can seem a simple and relatively unimportant act in your life can have huge ramifications in the world and can lead to the fulfillment of your destiny.

Fulfilling your destiny leads right on from fulfilling your potential. You could say that the two go hand in hand. So whether you focus on your potential or your destiny it doesn't really matter, what is important is, that you manage to experience and achieve all that you can during your stay here on Earth. Everything has a purpose, a potential if you like, and it must expand into that potential to complete its cycle.

"What a man can be, he must be. This need we may call self-actualization...It refers to the desire for self-fulfilment, namely, to the tendency for him to become actualized in what he is potentially. This tendency might be phrased as the desire to become more and more what one is, to become everything that one is capable of becoming."
Abraham Maslow—American Psychologist

In the quote above Maslow used the term self-actualization when speaking about our potential and he listed the following characteristics of what he called self actualised people.

Spontaneous in taking action and making decisions
Interested in solving problems.
Creative in work, family, social, and recreational pursuits.
Close with other people – strong support network (but not a vast one)
Strong morality system.
Objective perspective, without prejudice.
Focused energy on one particular task: their calling or mission in life..
View the world with a sense of awe and wonder.
May have peak experiences of intense joy and wonder that leaves them feeling inspired and transformed.

In order to reach these conclusions Maslow studied such greats as Albert Einstein, Abraham Lincoln and Eleanor Roosevelt. In other words, successful people who had achieved greatness in their lives. Well, we might not be an Einstein or a Lincoln but what is really important here is that we, during our lifetime, manage to fulfil our own unique potential and come to realise who we truly are.

HOW TO BECOME SELF-ACTUALIZED

Be honest and open with your thoughts and feelings. This is more easily said than done but if we can drop the fear and the facades that we hide behind, if we can be real and genuine and congruent (that is to say, our internal thoughts and behaviours are totally in sync with our external actions) then we can begin to grow into who we truly are.

If you can get rid of your judgements, and love and accept someone for who they truly are, if you can value people even if you know their failings and their dark side, then this is also hugely beneficial in reaching your goal.

Finally, if you can relate to another's emotions and experiences and be empathic enough to put yourself in another's shoes then you are getting there.

In other words, if we can nurture genuineness, acceptance, and empathy these qualities will help us to become self-actualized, find our true calling, and fulfil our potential in life. Remember your destiny might not lie in discovering a new planet, finding a cure for cancer or saving the world from global warming but, whatever it is, if you can do it with your heart and soul then you will achieve what you set out to achieve, and who is to say that the smallest deed doesn't, in the end, have the greatest impact.

One last tip, in order to become self actualised and fulfil your destiny it is crucial that you participate in Life and do something that adds value to other people or the planet.

COMMITMENT

"Until on is committed
There is hesitancy, the chance to draw back,
Always ineffectiveness.

Concerning all acts of initiative (and creation)
There is one elemental truth,
The ignorance of which kills countless ideas
And splendid plans:

That the moment one definitely commits oneself,
Then Providence moves too.

All sorts of things occur to help one
That would otherwise never have occurred.

A whole stream of events issues from the decision,
Raising in one's favour all manner
Of unforeseen incidents and meetings
And material assistance,
Which no man could have dreamt
Would come his way.

I have learned a deep respect
For one of Goethe's couplets:

Whatever you can do, or dream you
can....begin it
Boldness has genius, power and magic in it."

W.N Murray
Scottish Himalayan Expedition 1951

BODY CYCLES
THE ENERGETICS OF COMPLETION

We have looked at the importance of completion in relation to finishing projects and ventures, how manifestation is just another form of completion and how important it is to find closure in our relationships and complete our lifes' work by fulfilling our potential, but before I finish I would like us to take a look at yet another form of completion. In the beginning of the book I mentioned that completing things was, among other things, essential for our health and wellbeing. When we can't find a solution to the problems that are stopping us from finishing our project and our usual strategies don't seem to be working we can grow more and more frustrated, helpless and anxious as time goes on. When we are anxious, which, incidentally, is often associated with procrastination, then we find our inability to make decisions greatly reduced. This in turn leads on to feelings of powerlessness and anger, with the accompanying physical manifestations, such as headaches, digestive disorders and back pain. You see where this is going? Finding a solution to our dilemma and sorting out our problems in order to get completion and release all that stuck energy is therefore vital to our health.

There is another aspect to completion, or rather the effects that non-completion has on us. Every time that we feel the impulse to reach out and hug someone, or run away from a situation, or get up and dance and we don't do it, that impulse gets lodged somewhere in our body as a tension. The more we block the complete expression of these naturally occurring impulses the tighter and more restricted our body becomes. A continuously blocked impulse to hug, for instance, which we may do out of fear or embarrassment, can transform into holding in the shoulders and arms that can eventually lead to restriction of movement and pain.

The same goes for the times that we had a need to express something verbally and for what ever reason we stifled it. Every unexpressed cry, laugh or shout gets set in the musculature of the jaw where it sits until our jaw seizes, our neck becomes like rock and our teeth are ground way to tiny stumps. Okay, I know this is an extreme example, but I want to make the point. Those frozen impulses will always be seeking ways to get free and complete themselves in expression. The trouble is that they can often escape at inopportune moments or in destructive habitual behaviours so that they damage not only our body but sometimes our psyche and the people around us as well. If you don't believe me then notice how you feel the next time that you get really angry and you don't express that anger.

You have all probably noticed that often sports people, especially those involves in racket sports, but also perhaps golfers and cricketers, will often play a phantom stroke after playing a poor one. Maybe they tightened up just before the point of impact or they were momentarily distracted so that the stroke does not play through cleanly. In other words, it fails to complete properly. By playing a 'pretend' stroke they are letting go of the restriction they feel, playing through as it should be played and freeing themselves to play that complete stroke next time.

If we think again about cycles in relation to completion we can see how in order to move out and explore our world we need to be open to receiving impulses back from the world. In other words, we step out, as it were, into a new situation and then wait for the feedback. The feedback that we get determines our next step. This is how we learn. If we just kept doing things without noticing the feedback that we get to our actions, then not only will we continue to make mistakes, but we will not learn and we will stunt our ability to adapt. If we can't adapt then we leave ourselves open to stress and we stunt our potential. So an impulse or movement that we make is always followed by a response which dictates our next action. This is the second part of the cycle. As we receive this feedback, that completes that cycle and we are ready to begin a new cycle and so on.

Nowhere is this cycle more simply and eloquently portrayed than in the Chinese Yin -Yang symbol. Here energy moving outward is balanced by energy moving back in. The energy expands in a Yang outward phase, reaches the extent of its flow and then changes direction to flow back inward in its Yin phase. This constant movement of outward and inward energy creates an eternal cycle of movement which is mimicked in our body. In our nervous system, for instance, where motor impulses are balanced with sensory feedback. We see it every time we reach out for something to eat and then bring it back into our mouth. We recognise it in the circulation of our blood as it goes out through the arteries from the heart and then returns through the veins. We feel it in the beating of our heart and the breathing of our lungs as they expand and then contract.

These complete cycles are going on in our body all the time and we don't even notice. One example is the circadian rhythms. There is a circadian rhythm for digestion which consists of three distinct phases.

1) Elimination   (of body wastes)   4am-12pm
2) Appropriation   (eating and digestion) 12pm-8pm
3) Assimilation   (absorption and use)   8pm-4am

It is perfectly possible, and indeed a common habit of ours, to interrupt any of these cycles but there are consequences. It is not only vital that each cycle completes itself before the next cycle can begin but that we take notice of these cycles and behave appropriately. In the instance of the circadian rhythms above we know how our body and our emotions can be skewed by eating a large meal late at night or skipping meals during the day.

Another circadian rhythm which can reek havoc with us if it is disturbed is the one related to sleep patterns. The sleep/wake cycle is dependent, in large part, on light and temperature and a change in either of these can upset the cycle. There are many health problems associated with a disturbance in the sleep circadian rhythm. These include Seasonal Affective Disorder (SAD) where the rhythm is disturbed due to the change in length of day and reduced sunlight, delayed sleep phase syndrome (DSPS) which is caused by a circadian rhythm abnormality causing the sufferers body to want to sleep later than normal. This one is familiar to every teenager on the planet! More temporary problems include jet lag and problems caused for those working late shifts. Temporary or not, disturbances in our natural rhythmic cycles can and do make us feel bad.

So, day after day, moment after moment, whether we acknowledge them or not, our bodies are going through their natural cyclic functions to make sure that we operate at maximum efficiency. Each cycle plays its part and as with all things there is a beginning to the cycle, a middle and an end. As I said, wheels within wheels, a microcosm mimicking the cycle of the seasons, the turning of the years and the spinning of the planets. A seemingly endless array of beginning and completing and beginning - each completion of the cycle marking the beginning of the next in a flawless continuous dance.

Everything in the Universe consists of energy and energy has the prime directive of movement. Without movement there is no life. Everything in our body from the activity of our heart to the pulsation of the tiniest cell is aquiver with vibrating, pulsating energy. Each energetic impulse has a cycle that it must follow until it is complete. Each phase of expansion must be followed by a period of contraction. We can see this in the energy line of our own lives. The energy that we are born with expands into childhood and adolescence until we mature as individuals (at least physically) and then, as that expansive phase completes, we begin to head into middle and then old age as the contractive phase of the energetic cycle comes in. It is a cycle that we cannot escape even though many of us try really hard to do so.

If energy has a natural propensity to expand and contract it stands to reason that sometimes it can get stuck at some point in the cycle. There are, for instance, some individuals who constantly express; who constantly give out energy and work to extremes, who tend to be extrovert and constantly engaged with the world. Conversely, there are individuals whose energy is more contractive, who shy away from external contact; are introvert and live out their lives in some inner reality world. Both these extremes are all well and good, for a while, but they do go against the natural order and sooner or later, as we see depicted so elegantly in the yin yang symbol, things will switch over into their opposite eventually. Take something to its extreme and the tension created will ensure that it snaps back.

This common occurrence means that the driven, highly motivated, go getting individual is heading for trouble unless they are very careful. Keep pushing that energy out and something has to give eventually. For the individual caught in the contracted phase of the energy, the danger is that too much introversion will eventually lead to isolation and phobias. Unfortunately, as we move further and further away from Life's natural cycles we are going to find ourselves more and more on the receiving end of this 'snap back' of energy. If only we could get in tune with the natural order, we would recognise that there are times when we need to move out and expand into the world and times when we need to retreat and recoup our energy ready for the next round. Within our birth/death cycle we experience thousands of mini cycles. If we could move through these without resistance, and revel in the natural cycles then Life would be as natural as breathing.

Fighting against these natural impulses is a sure fire way to bring about physical discomfort and stress us out. We find ourselves frustrated, tense and anxious and often disconnected from family and friends. Fighting against the natural impulse to complete the things we begin in Life means that among the casualties are our bodies, minds and spirit.

MORE STRATEGIES TO GET YOU TO YOUR GOALS

SWOT ANALYSIS

In the chapter entitled To Start or not To Start, I suggested that employing a SWOT analysis could be useful. SWOT stands for Strengths, Weaknesses, Opportunities and Threats. Identifying your strengths and weaknesses as well as the opportunities available to you and any threats that might hamper your progress is a great way to start any project.

STRENGTHS

Make a list of the strengths that you possess that will help with your venture. These can be practical things such as good computer skills, a good design eye, or character traits such as determination, honesty or good communication skills. If you are stuck on what to write down, ask a friend. Sometimes it can be hard to acknowledge what we are good at or conversely we can be deluded about our level of skills. Get your friend to give an honest viewpoint.

WEAKNESSES

Admitting to your weaknesses requires a long, hard, honest look at yourself but believe me it is best to do so at this stage or you are bound to come unstuck later on. Weaknesses can be such things as an inability to work alone, problems with concentration or poor time management skills. Look at these things in relation to your project and acknowledge how they might hinder your progress.

OPPORTUNITIES

When it comes to opportunities for your venture these can be related to time planning, *"I can do this now that the children are off to college."* Sometimes the opportunity in a business venture means seeing an opening for what you plan to produce, a niche in the marketplace or the chance opportunity to hook up with a friend who you feel good about working with and with whom you can pool resources.

THREATS

Ok, I realise this sounds intense and unless your project is to launch a new street drug that will attract the attention of the mob, threats in this context mean things like personal conflict with family who may make demands on your time and attention thus threatening your ability to get the job done. Watch out for the subtle yet deadly threat of self sabotage. That small sinister voice in your head saying things like, *"You will never achieve this, you have always been hopeless at this."*

Once you have completed your lists, make sure that those things you have listed under strengths are those things that will actually help with the project that you have in mind. Take a particular look at what you have put under threats and weaknesses and see what you can do to eliminate them. If you have difficulty working alone, then see if you can find a friend or colleague who is willing to work alongside you, or join a group venture. If your project is to make a pottery vase it can be more fun and more encouraging to do it in a pottery class than struggling alone at home for instance. As for threats, these are often more difficult to resolve but that shouldn't stop you trying. Demands on your time can be negotiated and even that wicked self depreciating voice in your head can have the volume turned down.

BIG PICTURE

After you have made your assessments, finished your swot analysis and eliminated possible weaknesses and threats, you are ready to give your venture the 'Go Ahead.' At this point it is good to get down a general outline on what it is you want to achieve. Jot down the major points. Be specific, and very clear on what it is that you actually want to achieve without getting bogged down in the detail at this stage. A 'ball park' schematic as it were. You don't have to get into major details right from the word go. In fact, it is better not to as you can just end up tying yourself in knots and getting thoroughly confused.

RESOURCES

Take another look at the honest notes of any skills that you do not have to get the job done and list where you might be able to access them. This could be as simple as reading a book to getting outside help with a certain aspect of the project.

DEADLINE

Next its a good idea to set a deadline. That way your project is less likely to run on for months or even years or, worse still, end up in the bin. Be realistic but firm with yourself. Sometimes, it helps to tell people what you are doing. That way you will stay focussed and motivated as they will keep asking you how it is coming along and you will not want to face the embarrassment of telling them that it is still at stage one after six months.

It goes without saying that the bigger the project then the more aware of the deadline you have to be. A big complex project can feel really overwhelming so it is best to chunk it down. Set yourself multiple deadlines along the way, i.e, by the end of the month I will have completed this aspect, by Christmas I will have completed the next and so on. Make a checklist so that you can tick off each chunk as you complete it. That way on those days when you feel like you are getting nowhere and achieving nothing you can look a the list and acknowledge the progress you have made. I find that scoring through an item as I complete it is more satisfying than just ticking it off. See what works best for you.

GET HELP

Finally don't be afraid to ask for help if you feel out of your depth or that deadline is looming large. If you feel that your self initiated project is really floundering go back and look and ask yourself what you could do to get started again. If you really find yourself going off track, you could try employing a coach, someone who will contact you regularly and give you a good talking to in order to keep you motivated and keep the project proceeding. I find a nagging partner can work just as well !

If you can't afford paid help, people are often happy to get involved in a small way for nothing. For larger schemes you could even try a bit if bartering. *"How about I cut the lawn for you if you will cast your expert eye over my plans and give me feedback?"*

MAPPING OUT A PATH

Another way to assess a project and see if you consider whether it is worth your time and attention is to mind map it. Mind Mapping was developed by Tony Buzan in the 1970's, and it alleviates the need to make endless and ultimately confusing, lists and notes. A good Mind Map is a visual representation, in this case, of your whole project and it shows the 'shape' of the subject, the relative importance of individual points, and the way in which facts relate to one another. If you are the kind of person who likes to 'see' what they are planning and 'get the look of it', in other words a very visual person, then mind mapping is definitely for you.

Because you are only taking up one side of paper, rather than having to flick through pages of notes and lists, then associations can be easily made. If, when you have drawn your map, you find out more information as time goes on, then you can easily add it in to the whole picture.

MIND MAPS ARE USEFUL FOR

Summarizing information.
Consolidating information from different sources.
Thinking through complex problems.
Presenting information in a format that shows the overall structure of your subject.

What's more, mind maps are very quick to review as you can often refresh information in your mind just by glancing at one. They engage much more of your brain in the process of assimilating and connecting facts, compared with conventional notes. They tap into the natural way in which our brain works by association and pattern recognition rather than by storing long lists on a myriad of different topics and finally, but more importantly

THEY ARE FUN !

Let's take a look at how you begin mapping out your idea. I like to draw my maps on paper but if you prefer to work on your computer then there are programmes such "The Brain" which will help you to mind map your project.

To begin your map, start with a big piece of paper, I find the bigger the better, and write the name of the project in the centre of it. If you like, instead of writing down the name, you can draw a picture to represent it. Then start drawing lines from this centre project into boxes, or more pictures if you prefer, to represent the various parts of the project. Like the branches of a tree you will find that your map will grow and spread as you continue drawing lines from individual boxes. Just make sure that you keep all the points that are relevant to a particular box, together. You can even colour code them. That way your planning doesn't degenerate into a messy plan and you can see the interconnectedness of everything.

For instance, say you want to start keeping chickens. Assuming that you have never done this before there is lots to think about and plan for. Your basic mind map might end up looking something like the one opposite. Once you have this then you can start adding in the detail. Certain aspects, like breed types and feed suppliers, may need researching. When you find out what you need you can add it to the map so more branches will appear. Remember it is your mind map so it will grow organically and work to suit your mind

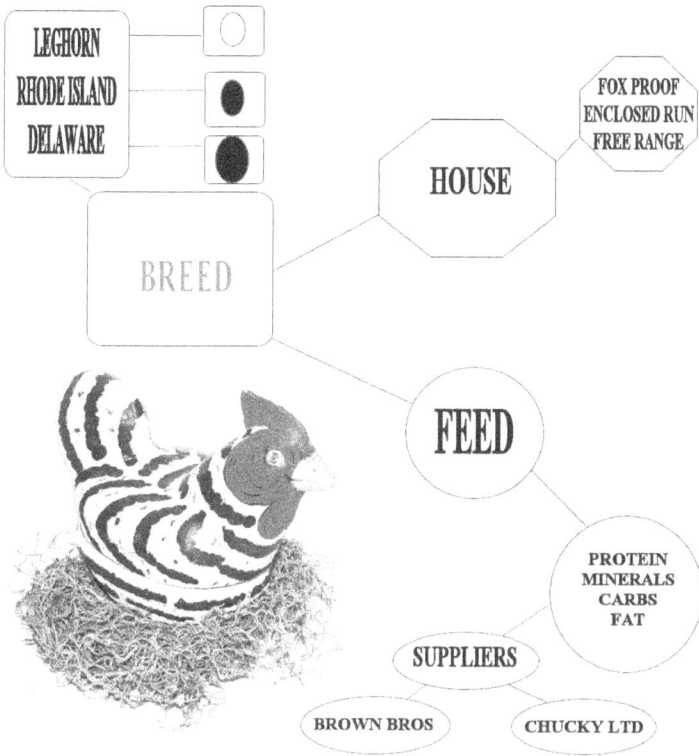

LEGHORN
RHODE ISLAND
DELAWARE

BREED

HOUSE

FOX PROOF
ENCLOSED RUN
FREE RANGE

FEED

PROTEIN
MINERALS
CARBS
FAT

SUPPLIERS

BROWN BROS

CHUCKY LTD

and how you uniquely process information. When you understand how to make notes in the Mind Map format, you can develop your own ideas to take them further.

KEEP IT SIMPLE

Single words or short phrases are best. You don't need an excess of words as they just clutter the map, and remember a picture can paint a thousand words so use them. Pictures can help you to remember information more effectively than words. Be creative.

USE COLOUR TO SEPARATE DIFFERENT IDEAS

This will help you to separate ideas where necessary and helps with organising the subject. If everything to do with one aspect of your project is in the same colour it is quick and easy to see what must be done. Colour coding is efficient, adds impact and it makes your map look cool.

USING CROSS-LINKAGES

Information in one part of the Mind Map may relate to another part. Here you can draw in lines to show the cross-linkages. This helps you to see how one part of the subject connects with another.

Mind Mapping has been proven to improve organisational skills by helping you to plan and organise your thinking before you start a project. You are less likely to get stuck along the way as, like all maps, if you get lost. it will point the way.

Once your mind map is completed then you are free to begin your project. You can see clearly what needs to be done in order to achieve your end result. Personally, as I complete each aspect of my map, each deadline if you like, I cross it out and then it is clear what I still have to do. This way I can see myself making real progress which helps to keep my enthusiasm for the project alive. I also give myself permission to make minor changes as I go along. Although the map for this book illustrated opposite, represents my initial plan, I was happy to adapt it as I went, but the clear format and interlinking kept me on track.

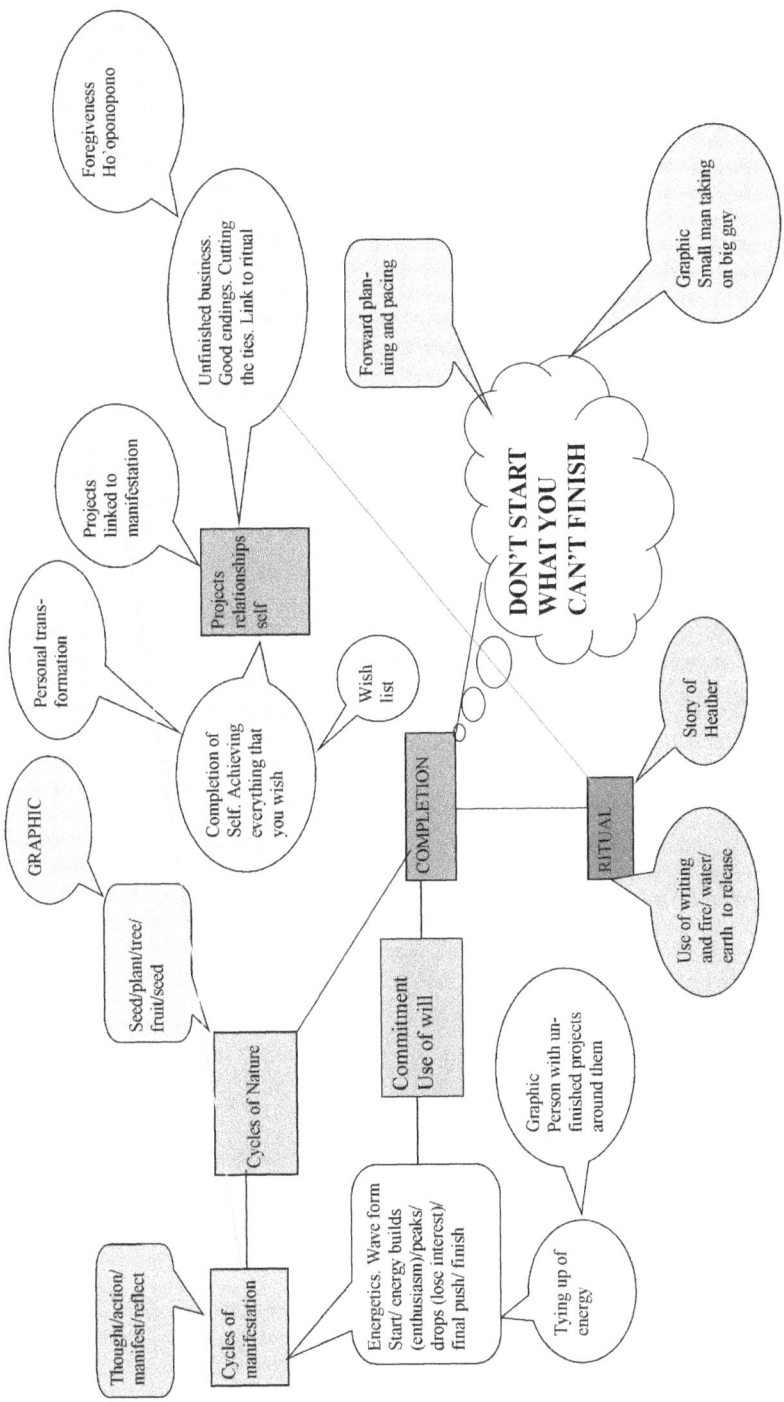

DON'T START WHAT YOU CAN'T FINISH

- Foregiveness Ho'oponopono
- Unfinished business. Good endings. Cutting the ties. Link to ritual
- Forward planning and pacing
- Graphic Small man taking on big guy
- Projects linked to manifestation
- Projects relationships self
- Personal transformation
- Completion of Self. Achieving everything that you wish
- Wish list
- GRAPHIC
- Seed/plant/tree/fruit/seed
- COMPLETION
- Story of Heather
- RITUAL
- Use of writing and fire/ water/ earth to release
- Cycles of Nature
- Thought/action/manifest/reflect
- Cycles of manifestation
- Commitment Use of will
- Graphic Person with unfinished projects around them
- Energetics. Wave form Start/ energy builds (enthusiasm)/peaks/ drops (lose interest)/ final push/ finish
- Tying up of energy

MORE MIND CONTROL

Here is a further suggestion for dealing with those not so helpful thoughts that arise from time to time.

Sit reasonably upright, with your head balanced on the spine. Feel that you are sitting on a hill top, facing the blue sky. You are relaxed and content. Feel that in your lap you have a cloth filled with pebbles. As you sit there, a thought comes into your mind. Mentally, pick up a pebble from the cloth and throw it, with the thought, away down the hill and say to yourself "*not wanted.*" Feel the satisfaction as each pebble rolls away from you.

Repeat this process with each troublesome thought that arises. Do this regularly and you will find that these thoughts trouble you less and less. You are withdrawing your energy and your support from them.

BE THE BEST YOU CAN BE

Sometimes we have a sense of who we would like to be or who we are capable of being but it seems a big stretch to get there. Here is a simple exercise that can help.

Firstly, choose the quality that you feel will be most helpful for realizing your potential. It can be anything, courage, grace, compassion, the list is endless. Choose the one that is most significant to you at this time.

Now, imagine yourself having that quality. Allow an image of yourself expressing this quality to take shape in great detail. Notice how you stand, the expression on your face, any gestures that you might be making. See yourself in as much details and clarity as possible. Do not worry if it is difficult to hold the image at first or it appears fuzzy, persevere.

When you can see yourself clearly expressing the quality that you wish for imagine yourself walking into the image and becoming one with it. As you merge with the image feel it infusing you with the desired quality. Feel the quality filling your whole body, experience it infusing your thinking, your whole being.

Then, imagine yourself expressing this quality, this new you, in an everyday situation in your life. Play around with different scenarios in which you express more of this quality than you have ever done before. Imagine this situations in as much detail as possible.

Repeat the exercise as many times as you wish but especially at those times when you feel your resolve flagging.

MAKING GOOD DECISIONS

One of the major problems that we can have in life is making good decisions. So often something happens to make us sad, upset, angry or frustrated and we feel that we have to do something about the situation in that moment. Making a good decision when you are feeling any of these strong emotions does not usually auger well. We then find ourselves regretting the decision that we made and more often than not having to change it to a better one at a later date.

So, never try to make a good decision when you are a negative space. Bad moods make for bad decisions. Never make decisions when you have insufficient information for a meaningful decision. You just end up second guessing and often guessing wrong.

Give yourself the time to think decisions through thoroughly. Even what seems a really good solution to a problem at the time may not work out well in the long run. Give yourself time to consider the issue. Sleep on it.

It always makes far more sense to make those important, and maybe even those not so important decisions, when you feel good. Therefore, the next time you find yourself in a situation where you need to make a decision try the process below.

Get comfortable. Close your eyes, and see what you were seeing, and feel what you were feeling, at a time in your life when something really wonderful happened. Notice where in your body the feeling starts, then where does it go? Maybe it starts in your abdomen and then moves upwards, or spreads out throughout your whole body? Just notice the path it takes.

Then, notice where it peaks, in other words where the wonderful feeling is most intense, and then notice where it goes away. Does it reverse direction or does it just slowly fade? Notice how it happens for you.

Now re-evoke that good feeling again and when the feeling reaches its peak take it and put it in the centre of your chest. Now keep bringing it round from wherever it peaks, and feels most intense, to your heart. Do it faster and faster until it gets more and more intense and the feeling spreads throughout your whole body. Now, think about the situation that you have to make a decision about. In this wonderful moment of peak experience the decision you make now will be the best you can make.

THE END

Now I am basking in the satisfaction of having completed my task of finishing this book. Its conception grew out of an inspiration in the early hours of one winter morning in that twilight zone between night and day and between sleep and wakefulness. I have come to realise in my own life just how vital completion is and the effects that incompletion can have on us at every level, from the physical right through to the very subtle layers of our existence. I hope I have at the very least persuaded you to think about the concept of completion in your own life, and at most, to fully embrace it and set about completing all those niggly things in your life that have been left undone.

When you do, you will be glad you did. You will have more energy, a clearer mind and a more relaxed body. What's more you will sleep better, wake more rested and ready to take on any challenge that life throws your way.

If that is not a powerful way to live your life then I don't know what is!

NOW WHAT'S THE FIRST THING ON YOUR LIST THAT

YOU

HAVE TO COMPLETE?

COMPLETING

"What is fragile is easy to break;

What is minute is easy to disperse.

Deal with a thing before it comes into existence;

Regulate a thing before it gets into confusion.

The common people in their business (or affairs and doings)

often fail on the verge of succeeding.

Take as much care with the end as you do with the beginning,

And you will have no failure."

Tao Te Ching

Acknowledgements

Abraham Maslow

Matthew McKay, Martha Davis, Patrick Fanning, 'Art of Cognitive Stress Intervention'

Piero Ferrucci 'What We May Be'

Trevor Leggett 'The Old Zen Master'

Buckminster Fuller 'Critical Path'

Richard Bandler 'An Evening with Richard Bandler'

VISIT

www.bookofcompletion.com

www.sinktherelationship.com

Other titles by Morag Campbell

Sink the Relation Ship (see extract p.106)

Earthkind

Quinta Essentia

A Promise Kept

The Power of Love

Available from

www.mwipublishing.com
www.masterworksinternational.com
and all good bookstores

Other titles from MasterWorks International

Quinta-Essentia
by Morag Campbell

A study of the Five Natural Elements and.how they all affect our lives even today.

A Promise Kept
by Morag Campbell

Autobiographical account of a profound spiritual adventure set in England and ancient Hawaii.

The Power of Love - A Guide to Consciousness and Change
by Phil Young and Morag Campbell

The ancient Polynesian viewpoint on spiritual development retold for the modern world.

The Way of the FlameKeeeper
by David Kala Ka La

A no punches pulled account of a personal spiritual journey

Polarity Therapy - Healing with Life Energy
by Alan Siegel ND and Phil Young

A clear extensively illustrated instruction manual in this unique healing art of energy balancing..

Earthkind
by Morag Campbell

There is something for everyone in this light-hearted fairy tale with a strong ecological theme

The Art of Mental Wellbeing - The Polarity Of Mental Wellbeing and Mental Disorder beyond the Medical Approach
by Tony Caves
An exploration of sacred geometry and energy in relation to mental health.

Mindessence - The Polarity of Life and Death
by Tony Caves
Ideas and methods to move beyond the notion of Life and Death and realise our true nature.

Sink the Relation Ship - Transform the Way you Relate
by Morag Campbell
A humorous, yet hard hitting look, at the problems that arise as a result of the way that we think about relationships. Contains practical suggestions for improving the way we relate.

Available from

www.mwipublishing.com
www.masterworksinternational.com
and all good bookstores

Extract from
SINK THE RELATION SHIP

WHAT ARE YOU WILLING TO DUMP OVERBOARD IN ORDER TO RELATE BETTER?

So we now know that when you relate to another person through an externalised Relation Ship, Partner Ship or Marriage that you lose direct contact with each other. The Relation Ship acts as a filter or a buffer to what is really going on.

Ensuring that you relate exclusively to the other person in the moment means that you can gain real insight and understanding into what is really going on for them and they can achieve the same with you. You establish such a strong connection that it can sometimes feel like you are in a bubble, cocooned from the outside world while you really get to know this person.

As well as dumping the need to make the other person wrong, giving up being angry at the other person, and being willing to give up all resentment and the need to punish the other person, there is one other condition that both parties need to embrace before they proceed and that is that each person has to take 100% responsibility for any mess that they find themselves in. By that I mean that if the way that we relate to another person is problematic or non existent, we each have to admit to it being 100% our fault. It is not the other person's fault. It is not our fault. It is not 50% their fault and 50% our fault, it is 100% for each of us. So there has to be 100% culpability and 100% determination from each of you to change things and really get clear and honest with the other person about the situation.

Scary? You bet!
Worthwhile? Absolutely!

Are you willing to take 100% responsibility today?

Once you are willing to dump all of these things, take total responsibility for the way you relate and acknowledge that hiding in the Relation Ship does not work then you are ready to begin more open and honest relating. When communication through the Relation Ship becomes two way communication just between two people it immediately becomes much more direct. One to one means there is less chance of misunderstanding and more chance of a meaningful conversation.

DUMB BELLS AREN'T SO DUMB

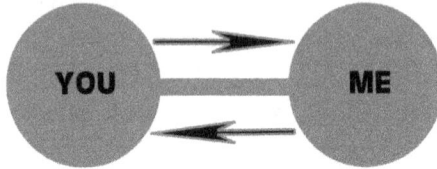

THEY BUILD BALANCE AND STRENGTH

Communicating in this way means that two people can connect in multiple ways, be that from the intellectual level, from the emotional, from direct experience or the spiritual. Being totally present, that is being in the here and now and paying attention to the other person, ensures that you stay really connected and that helps to carry a continuous stream of conscious and unconscious information between you. In the heat of emotionally charged conversations, where one or both parties can feel vulnerable and raw, this connection maintains a safety net that keeps each of them from falling apart. This purer form of communication is toned down and diluted when 'The Relation Ship' becomes involved.

So we now need to look at a better way of starting and maintaining the connection that we want with another person - a way of relating that is more meaningful and fulfilling for everyone.